Mommies Making Money!

So.... You have decided it is time to make money, but how? You have tried the workplace, but you are always getting called home for sick children. The daycare provider is taking home more than you, and your baby looks at you and cries as you leave her with the sitter, and her latest runny nose. There has got to be another way, and there is! This book will help Mommies make money. Whether you need to just supplement your husbands money, or you need to make a living, this book will give you practical solutions that really work. These solutions will flow with your life and teach your children important work ethics.

Start where you are at.

If you are a working mother, do not quit until you feel comfortable with these solutions. I started with selling children's clothes on Ebay. I knew clothes, so when I was out at the yard sales, I would pick up very cheap clothing, and sell them on Ebay. I found that I could take something that I paid a Quarter or fifty cents for, and turn it into more money. The only problem is it takes time to list on Ebay, so rather than make hundreds of dollars, I was only making tens of dollars. I looked for successful Ebay sellers, and started looking for the items that they sold and started selling them. You can actually decide when you are out whether you want to make $10.00 that day or

$100.00 on the choices of items you buy and sell. I also know that you have to work with in your means. If you only have quarters to start with, then use quarters. I find on the times that I have quarters, old board games are great. They usually bring in between $9.99 -$45.00 depending on the game. I take the time to see if they look complete. I also look to see what they are. Milton Bradley and Parker Brothers usually make good money. The game "Hotels" if complete will bring in $45.00. Start where you are at, and build from there. As your knowledge increases, so will your profits. Give yourself the time to learn. Rejoice over your successes, even the small ones. You are one step closer to your future of a better financial future. As my knowledge grew, and so did my money, I found it much easier to find 5 great items that will make more money, that spending quarters and dollers to make less. It works like this: You are out at a yard sale and the most beautiful clothes are only a quarter each. Wow!!! Right next to them is a beautiful Old Saxaphone in an old smelling case For $25.00 Hmmmmmmmmm. Pick the Sax!!!!!!!! The clothes would bring in about $20.00 and you have to take pictures of all of them. The Sax will sell for about $125.00 unles. You will get good at this!

Chapter 1: Getting Set Up

Three years ago, I realized we needed extra money, and I could not afford to leave and go to work because the high cost of daycare for mutiple children! I have 8 children, 6 still at home and 3 children 5 and under. I thought about working nights again, waitressing, but I knew that would be a lot of hard work and to many hours! I also could use the college degree I earned, but then I would be gone all day from my still very young children!

So many people were talking about selling on Ebay, so I decided I would try it. The first thing I needed was a computer. The cost for this was around $500.00. It took time for me to come up with this, but after a few months I did. The step was to register on Ebay. Ebay is great about teaching people how to sell. Set aside about 2 hours to go through the tutorial. It will walk you through from start to finish. I would reccomend at night when the kids are sleeping, or when they are taking a nap, so you can really concentrate on this. They have a step by step process that will lead you through easily, and after I registered on Ebay, I registered on Paypal. Most people on Ebay like to use Paypal. They can pay for their items right away. Paypal will also walk you through this.

Once you are set up with Ebay and Paypal, you will need to purchase a good Digital Camera. They are about $89.00 - $99.00. They will bring back all your money back in the first couple of sales!

Chapter 2
Work can be fun!!!!
Who said work is work. I look forward to sneaking off on a Saturday morning before anyone is awake and being the first one in the neighborhood to do spy on the set up
of my favorite part...Yard Sales!!
Do your Homework the night before. The Sales I love are "moving Sales" Neighborhood Sales are awesome too! Some of the Greatest sales also are

church rummage sales. The items have been donated so it is easy to price things low, so they sell!! If you are trying to build up inventory this is a great way. At the end of the sales they have "bag" sales. I go to the same church sale every year, and I go 15 minutes before the bag sale starts. I walk around and collect in a pile what I am going to buy. Then when the time comes, I purchase my bag, and usually it is the biggest bag, I fill up my bag, and then go home with tons of treasure! I love these sales, and Love to buy!!

The very very best sale I
have ever been to was on my
birthday! I told my husband
I was going to what is called
an Estate Sale. These sales are
held by family or a hired person
to sell off all the belongings
of a deceased family member.
These sales are also held when
Grandma decides to move to
Florida. Then they are "living
Estate" Sales. Anyways, my
husband said "you have enouph
junk everywhere, you do not
need to go to that sale. Not
missing a beat, I reminded him
it was my birthday, and he was

getting paid that day. I did end up going with his blessings, and the items I bought are making incredible money as I write this write now. This estate sale was a Doctor and his wife and their 8 children which they saved everthing from childhood. This is exactly what people look for on Ebay!

###mommie moment: While working on Ebay, I asked my husband to watch the kids for a little while. My 3 year old asked for a snack, and then happily went back to my bedroom, sat on my bed with her snack, and fell asleep watching TV. She later woke up, and life went on...until I went to bed that night, putting my feet into the sheets, I realized that not only was it cold, but sticky. I asked my husband what is in the sheets??? He said, "Oh...I wondered where that popsicle went that Hannah was eating." Hmmmmmmmmm!!!!!!!!! Moral of this mommie moment, watch your husband watch the kids!!!

Chapter 3

What to buy

Buy what you know! Find Your niche! Everybody has something they love. As a mother of 8, I have studied my kids. They all love toys and hobbies, and video games, and outside climbers, and swingsets! This is my niche. I can take my kids with me and find these items very cheap at the yard sales and then sell them on Ebay. My Goal is to at least double my money, but more often than not, I can sell my item for more than 10 times the amount I bought them for.

Some of my biggest money makes are the Little Tikes Toys. They always sell! I have people stop by my house that see these toys outside, and offer me money for them all the time. I usually do not make as much as I would selling them on Ebay, but I move them much faster, and I do not have to ship which is nice.

Vintage Fisher Price is also a big money maker. I bought the old Fisher Price record player for $1.00 and just sold it for

$14.00. I find the old barns and silo's and Little People at yard sales and stick them on Ebay, and sometimes list them for $45.00 and sure enough, sombody wants it! They make good money.

Old Toys that you turn your nose up at the yard sales are Gold Mines! I found a truck load of old toys at that Estate sale! These old toys are what collectors are looking for. The more you start taking a little risk, the more you will find it is not that hard to strike gold! I found my "gold" at that estate sale!   I have a friend who went up to the attic in her garage and dug out some of her husbands old toys. His Mother had taken good care of them, and put them in the original box. She put them on Ebay, and some of these toys made $200-$350.00 per toy. Think Old Toys when you go to yard sales!

My brother is a professional pilot, who has even flew one of the president's. He has a love for old cars, snowmobiles, and old car parts. I think it makes his heart beat fast when he finds a car part that will make a lot of money. His niche is finding a few car parts that make a lot of money and putting them on Ebay. Everyone has something they know and love. There are so many others that share that same love, and do not know where to find what they are looking. They go to their computer and type in the "thing" they are looking for, even the search engine's will bring you right to the "item". You put that "thing" on. You have just made money,and sombodies day! I can not tell you the "Thank you's" I have gotten from people who could not believe I had what they wanted. I was at a church rummage I kept walking by this old baby toy. It was a yellow flat "crawligator" in the box. It was $1.00. I checked to see if it had the parts. It did. It sat in one of my storage spaces for one year. One night I was sick of looking at it so I stuck it on Ebay, because I just could not throw it away, which is what I almost did before going to bed. It was 11:00 pm, and that is a little late for me to list because their are people out their who actually sleep at night. The next morning it was getting bids. The ending bid was around $133.00. Who would have known that this was a rare sought out toy from the 80's, and to think, I almost threw it away! This happened another time with an outside toy that I bought from one of my Ebay Mentors. I bought it for $5.00, because that is what she paid, and she just wanted to get her money back. My kids played on it all summer. What it was was an outside Today's Kids Primary Colors Merry go around. It was faded, and had some cracks on it. At the end of the summer, I wanted to have my yard clean, so I stuck it on Ebay, hoping to make at least $10 - $15 on it. It went up to around $145.00. I could not beleive it, with defects and all! Sometimes I think "wow, I could be working at some job somewhere, making that in a week after paying Daycare for my small children, or I could continue to list on Ebay.

Another great place to find merchandise is the clearance racks and aisles. I have bought more toys on clearance, and then even that day stuck them on Ebay and doubled or tripled my money! This happened with the ESPN Game Center. I kept finding them at Walmart for $40.00. I bought 3. I sold one for around $99.00, and one for around 150.00. Clearance is great for winter jackets, backpacks, and tons of clothes. A place to store everything is imperative, because what most people who sell this on Ebay hold on to them for the season that they will make the most money! My oldest daughter made great money buying a coat on clearance, and even in the hot of summer she was able to make great money on that coat! She knew the brand was highly sought out after, so she bought it low, and sold it high!

A great start is your own home. There are treasures that you do not even know that they are valualbe! I can not count the times that I just decided with the help of my husband, that I would just start looking through our own garage,and find stuff to sell.

Chapter 4

More Money! Although Ebay is a great way to roll in the

dough from home, I also buy and sell from home. I actually bought 8 couches, yes, I said 8 couches from a Goodwill 50% off sale. My husband is a teacher, and the teachers got a great laugh when my husband told them in the teachers lounge what "Lucy" did. My husband calls me "Lucy" from the "I love Lucy" episodes. Anyways, Each of the couches cost about $35.00 and I sold each one of them for about$100-$150.00. That was a nice $1000.00 Who was laughing all the way to the bank, "Lucy". The best furniture to sell is bunkbeds. I look for bunkbeds in the $20 - $40.00 range. I find them either through local online resourses, or yard sales. I then call the newspaper and put an ad in for $100.00 - $300.00 depending on the set, and are mattresses included. If they are metal, $100.00. Solid wood, no mattresses $125.00 - $150.00. Used loft bunk beds sell for $300.00.

Mommie Moment: While grocery shopping with my 3

year old, Hannah, and 1 year Old Jenna, otherwise known as "RURU", all was well. Mom was pushing the really big grocery cart that had a built in car, and Hannah and RURU were driving. While checking out I noticed the grocery clerk giving me a dirty look. I could see the back of the kids, they looked fine, but the bagger was also giving me a dirty look. I chalked it up as irratable people, and went on with life. The bagger walked out into the very chilly 50 degree fall day still giving me a dirty look. I reached down to pick up my 1 year old, and to my horror, she was sitting there with no shirt on. She had ripped it off between aisle 7 -10. Embarrassed, I tried to explain to the grumpy grocery store bagger that she must have ripped her shirt off inside the store, and there was no way I was going to look for it because she would get colder. He smiled and then said "that is really funny"! I prayed they would find it, to save my reputation as MOM! A week later, I went back in and asked for the shirt. A puzzled customer standing next to me

said, " what happened???"
I shared the story, she laughed, and my reputation was saved for the moment. Hmmmmmmmmmm!!!
Chapter 5

Even More Money

Sometimes I go to storage unit auctions. I have done okay with these, and I know people who do awesome with these. There is lots of suprise in these, and sometimes you can get a lot of stuff for very little money! You have to not be afraid to bid. So many people go and just watch. You do have to clean out the entire storage unit within 2 days, but usually the storage people will work with you if you need more time. I have bought entire storage units for $5.00. I have found lots of money in pockets of the clothes that people put in these units before donating the clothes. It is hard work, and you do get a ton of stuff. If you have a barn, or storage area, this would be great for you. At one time I actually got a semi-trailer and put it on my property. The problem with this is you get so much stuff, you no longer no what to sell first and it gets to overwhelming with children. If you are organized and you can handle this than great! The rule of thumb is get rid of it in 30 days!

Regular Auctions are a great way to get a lot to sell for very little money. You can buy an entire line of "stuff" for sometimes $1.00. I do have freinds who love to do this. Some of the items I have acquired this way, have been very profitable. This is also how

I learned a lot about what sells on Ebay.

Overview

Garage Sales, and thrift shops are easy with children. Auctions are great if you want to accumulate a massive amount to sell with little money. They are hard with small children because you have to wait for the items you are bidding on to sell. If you go this route, bring a freind to help, or you and your freind trade off babysitting.

Chapter 6 The Spritual Aspect

Prayer Works!

Okay... I have to throw this in. I also pray alot. I do believe that

God wants me to be successful, and I believe he shows me many times what to buy. I have a freind who beleives this too. She will pray and ask God to show her exactly what to sell. She ends up making lots of money this way.

More Ways to accumulate inventory. I know what it is like to want to buy at all these yard sales, but not have any money to do this. That is why I will share with you these secrets that I share with many struggling mothers, who either are single, or they just do not have the means to buy to get started. I can not emphasize enough, start where you are!!!! People at the end of their yard sales are very tired, and are sick of looking at the same stuff that they have been starring at for 2-3 days. You are their rescue ranger! I can not tell you how wonderful it is to have some one take all your stuff at the end of their sale, and they did not even have to load it up in their minivan, and drive it to the donation box! This is how it is done. You go to the yard sales, especially the

moving ones. You hand them
a flyer or just your name and
number, and tell them that you
will gladly take any of their yard
sale leftovers. The flyer works
great, and they will most of the
time call you. Some will wonder
what your mission is. Just be
honest and tell them that you are
a mother making your income
from home. I also throw in that
whatever I do not sell, or can
not use, I will gladly donate to
charity. Sometimes, a group of
us mothers have gone together
to do this. It really works. You
will begin to accumulate all

sorts of stuff to sell. This is a good starting place. I also get the message out by word of mouth. The people who know me, know that I love Little Tikes toys, and love to sell them. They will call me and alert me to sales, or Little tikes out by the trash.

Okay....I have to throw in this little peice of info...I have been called Dr. Dumpster. We live in a throw away, move away society, so people really do throw wonderful things away. Colleges are great!!! Here are some of the things I have collected that were on their way to the great Landfill, and I am not Joking! 10 brand new Adias Backpacks, 6 of new with tags. This was at a huge University, that I live close to. The little Tikes Gourmet Kitchen, like new. We were driving down the road, when I spotted a man putting this kitchen out to the trash. I screamed in the car, scared my husband, got accused of being the queen of all trash, and my husband did the legal 180, so that I could have this treasure! Now, I have class. I asked the man who was obviously throwing this toy away, if he was throwing away this toy. He said "Yes", it was in the way of his new lawn mower in the garage and I could take it with blessings! I have also found that the garbage man comes on Tuesday for the major collage university in our town. I will drive thru sometimes Sunday night, or Monday and just "look" to see if there is anything worthy of stopping. I have found if it is worthy, people usually will put it by the dumpster because they want someone to take it. I 99% of the time would never take anything out of the dumpster, but I have to leave room for situations like this. I saw some huge boxes in a dumpster at a freinds store. I called him up and asked if I could have the boxes. He said "sure", and we were moving at the time so it worked out great. In the boxes were brand new clothes that still had the tags on them. I called him up and told him, and he said that these boxes came from a tenants house that no longer lived their. I was welcome to whatever was in the box. Another situation was my father, who is a real Doctor lived in a nice apartment complex. He was taking the trash to his dumpster and noticed 2 beautiful lamps in the dumpster. He reached into the dumpster and discovered that these lamps would match perfect with his decor. That is why I will leave the 1% margin, because there might be times.....

The Balance of working with kids

Balance is the key word. I can tell you that since I sat down to work on this book, I have been interupted about 10 times. My kids and my husband come before making money. I am use to stopping what I am doing, meeting the need of the moment and then going back to business. I know for some of you, this could drive you nuts! Being a mom means being flexible. I only feel stress when I myself am putting to many demands on my time to be a wife and a mother, and to try to make money from home. I will not lie to you, it is not easy. Sometimes, I get very frustrated and think, I wish I was like the person who does drop their kids off at the daycare, and then does her job. I have to do my "job" selling from home, and still be the mommie, and the wife. The secret is forming a schedule that works for you! I usually clean on Monday because Yard sales are Thursday through Saturday, and in our community Sunday. I always do laundry, night and day, but I do not always have time to fold it. I make money, so I can afford to call somebody, and pay them to help me catch up on housework. In my book, this is okay. I want to succeed, and I know I need help to get there. Ask for help when you need it , because when you are getting started, you will need lots of help. My children do so much to make money right by my side. Some of my children are great baby watchers! My son is great helping me set up the old board games, to check to see if their are missing peices. I use the strengths of each of the people in my life to help me, and in turn we are all helped. The extra money helps pay for the camps we could never afford before, or the 1/2 gallon of Chocolate milk, that I would normally not by, buy I love to bless my family. I love to give them the life experiences that money can by. It is not wrong to have money, and enjoy it! I am willing to work very hard for it, yet still balance the prioritys of being a wife and a mother are still getting done. Now I have freinds who think that I should do all my own housework, but that is their problem. I know I need help, and I ask all the time. I am becoming a better organized person, but still am a work in progress. I have a friend who is wonderful, and I do mean wonderful with housecleaning and folding! We need each other. Rather than beat myself up because I was up listing late the night before, I accept my mission. Ebay is providing a way right now!

Chapter 7 See The Need Fill the Need

Opportunity knocks every day! A young single mother stopped by my house to ask if I knew the number to a local

food bank. She was in need of groceries and diapers. She also commented on how a tornado of laundry had overtaken my living room. I called a service organziation for her, but she needed her social security card, which she would have to locate before receiving assistance.
In the mean time, I asked her would you like to make $40.00 and just help me clean. I had just taken 14 loads of laundry to the laundrymat because I reguraly get behind on laundry because of the huge family, and the one washer, and one

dryer! She was thrilled! She even came back the next day to help me straighten the bedrooms up. We both benefited. These opportunites are always there, be bold enouph to ask!

Chapter 8 Stay connected

The best success is in numbers. Sometimes I start to loose motivation, so I will call a friend to see what she has gotten lately to sell. The excited of the thrill of finding a Little Tikes Log Cabin House for $5.00, because the family is moving, and putting it on Ebay and selling it that afternoon for $150.00, is so awesome. These stories happen all the time, but you can not sit home and think it will come to you. You must get out! Freinds and Family will cheer you on and get excited when you succeed! This helps you to push forward. It makes putting the kids in the carseat and driving around to yard sales so worth it, when you are buying heaps of back to school clothes from one item that made $145.00. Sometimes when I feel discouraged or tired I just go outside, and start sorting through the stuff to list. The excitement will start to rise again as I find the great items that I bought to sell, but never got to it because I stuffed it in the garage, and forgot about it!

Chapter 9 Stay Organized Stay Organized!!!

The very first thing you should know is have a place to put your stuff the moment you pull into the driveway. My method was just throw it in the garage or big outdoor toys went out in the yard. I still made lots of money, but everything was a mess. I had extremely valuable items that I had no idea I had them because I had no system. The same freind that came over to help my tornado living room, also loves to organize my Ebay stuff in the garage. There are really people out there that like this kind of thing! The extra step of putting the items where they need to go is so important and vital to your success! If you are not good at it, chances are someone you know would love to use thier gifts and talents to help you! It is so worth it! The times that I have not

taken the extra step, things get
broken, or ruined and end up
in the dumpster. This happens
when I over-accumulate also.
When you start making money,
it is easy to just keep going out
and collecting more and more
and more. The problem is you
will collect 20 items on one
outing and list 5 of them on
Ebay, because that is all you
have time for, and then never
get around to putting the other
15 items on, before going out
and collecting 20 more. Some
weekends I do not go out yard
sailing just because I need to sell

what I have. This helps to stop the cycle of over-accumulation.

Chapter 10 Never Give Up

You can do this. You can be a mommie making money. Your kids can be your greatest helpers, and can learn how to be a very hard worker along side of you. You do not have to be a victim sitting in your living room wishing your kids had better clothes and toys. You can change your future today by just getting off the couch or telephone and changing you future. Just because you have the children does not mean your life is on hold. You can succeed right where you are, and right in the place in life you find yourself. The decision is will you dare to do something different.

www.ingramcontent.com/pod-product-compliance
Lightning Source LLC
Chambersburg PA
CBHW051246170526
45165CB00004B/1593

*9 7 8 1 4 4 0 4 9 6 1 5 8 *